GREAT SCIENTISTS
THOMAS EDISON

STEVE PARKER

Belitha Press

This edition published in 2002 by
Belitha Press
A member of Chrysalis Books plc
64 Brewery Road, London N7 9NT

Copyright © Belitha Press
Text © Steve Parker

Illustrations/photographs copyright © in this format
by Belitha Press

Typeset by Chambers Wallace, London
Printed in Malaysia

British Library Cataloguing in Publication Data
for this book is available from the British Library.

ISBN 1 84138 490 9

Acknowledgements

Photographic credits:
Bridgeman Art Library 17
Corbis 27
Cincinnati Historical Society/Robert Harding
    Picture Library 4
Mary Evans Picture Library title page, 13 top,
    19 left, 23 top, 24 top
Illustrated London News Picture Library
    25 bottom
The Image Bank 9 top right Jake Rajs,
The Library of Congress 6 right
Mansell Collection 16 bottom, 23 bottom,
    24 middle
National Portrait Gallery, London 8
Nelson Gallery, Atkins Museum, Kansas City/
    Robert Harding Picture Library 7

Peter Newark's American Pictures 6 left, 9 bottom
    right, 10, 12, 14 top, 16 top, 20, 22 bottom left,
    24 bottom
Ann Ronan Picture Library 21 top
Science Photo Library/J-L Charmet 13 bottom
US Department of the Interior, National Park
    Service, Edison National Historic Site 5 top,
    11 top, 22 top
US Department of the Interior, National Park
    Service, Edison National Historic Site/Robert
    Harding Picture Library 5 bottom, 9 left,
    11 bottom, 15 top, 21 bottom, 22 bottom right,
    25 top, 26

Cover montage images supplied by Mary Evans
Picture Library and Ann Ronan Picture Library

Illustrations: Tony Smith 14-15, 18
Rodney Shackell 19
Editor: Kate Scarborough
Designer: Andrew Oliver
Picture researcher: Vanessa Kelly

Contents

Introduction

Imagine what life would be like without electric lights, or record players, telephones, or the movies at the cinema. Imagine no power stations, or the pylons, cables and wires that bring electricity to our homes, factories, offices and schools.

Thomas Edison, the "greatest inventor of his age", was central to all these developments. In the years between about 1870 and 1920, Edison and his co-scientists came up with hundreds of useful devices and machines, mostly worked by electricity. They ranged from a giant kiln (oven) for making cement to one of the most familiar items in any home – the electric light bulb.

In fact, Edison himself rarely came up with a completely new invention. His talents lay in taking the ideas and inventions of others and improving them. His **engineering** and fault-finding skills made machinery more efficient and reliable. He showed how devices and processes could be used successfully on a large scale, to solve problems, to speed up communications and manufacturing, and generally to improve life.

An early photograph of Cincinnati, Ohio, taken in 1848 a year after Edison's birth. It shows a world of steam engines and gas lamps, so different from the world of electric light bulbs and motor cars that Edison left behind in 1931.

Chapter One

The Early Years

The house where Thomas Alva Edison was born in Milan, Ohio, 1847.

On 11 February 1847, in Milan, Ohio, USA, Thomas Alva Edison was born. His family lived in a small house near Lake Erie's shore. Thomas' father, Samuel, was in the timber business. He and his wife Nancy had seven children altogether, but three died young. When Thomas was a baby, his surviving brother and sisters were already teenagers.

A problem pupil

In 1854, at the age of seven, Thomas and his family moved near to Port Huron, on the southern tip of Lake Huron. His father's business had failed, and the family had little money. About this time Thomas caught scarlet fever, which left him very hard of hearing. The next year he had the only proper schooling of his life. But his great curiosity, poor hearing and tendency to play tricks soon got him into trouble. After only three months the schoolmaster said he was "retarded", and Nancy Edison took her son away from the school. No one suspected that Edison would be a multi-millionaire within 22 years.

Thomas at the age of 12 declared himself to be grown up and independent, so he took a job selling food and newspapers on the railroad.

A deserved reward

Edison remembered his days on the railroad as the happiest time of his life. His poor hearing meant he had trouble hearing normal speech. But he could hear passengers shouting above the noise of the train. And he could hear the high-pitched click of the telegraph machine as it printed out messages in the dots and dashes of **Morse code**.

He once rescued the young son of a telegraph agent at Mount Clements, a small station on the line. As a reward, he was taught how to work the telegraph machine. It was the beginning of his telegrapher career and his interest in electrical machines.

The home chemistry set

Nancy took over Thomas' education. He read books on **philosophy** and science, including one of the most famous science books of all time, Isaac Newton's *Principia*. This gave him great respect for scientific theories, but put him off mathematics! His imagination was caught mainly by chemistry and physics experiments. He set up a home laboratory in the household basement. He asked local shopkeepers for free jars and chemicals, and copied the experiments in science books.

In 1859, the Grand Trunk Railroad opened a line from Port Huron to Detroit. New railroads and **telegraphs** were snaking across the land. Thomas got a job as a newsboy, selling newspapers on the trains. He soon enlarged his first business by selling candy and seasonal vegetables as well! He employed other boys at stations along the line, and he made enough money to buy more science books. The boy scientist even used a spare wagon on the train as a laboratory and a printing works for the passengers' newspaper, *The Grand Trunk Herald*, which he wrote himself.

The coming of the telegraph

Sending messages over long distances was difficult in a huge country like the USA. When Edison was a boy, the Pony Express operated for a short while. Teams of riders and horses covered 3,200 kilometres, from Missouri to California, in 10 days. But messages sent as electrical signals along telegraph wires went at the speed of light and in 1861 the Pony Express went out of business.

Tramp telegrapher

The American Civil War began in 1861. The next year, the telegraph operator in Port Huron went off to fight, and Edison took his job. Between sending and receiving messages, he continued his experiments in the basement of the office. In 1864 he took a telegraph job in Canada.

This was the beginning of a six-year career as a wandering "tramp telegrapher". These men were fast, skilled telegraph operators and worked for whoever offered high wages. Edison roamed the USA and Canada. He liked to work on night shifts, so he could continue his scientific reading and experiments during the day. In some jobs, he got into trouble because he had ideas and made machines which showed up his bosses. Several times he had to leave.

Thomas would have worked on trains much like this one below. This picture was painted in 1860 when the trains and wagon trails were the main form of communication.

The importance of patents

A patent is a description of an invention which is registered and kept by the authorities, to show who thought of it first. For a set period of time afterwards, only the inventor can make, use or sell the invention. Or the inventor can give permission to others to do so, or sell the patent to others. Patents are very important if an invention becomes successful, because the person who owns the patent makes the money.

New uses for electricity

In 1868, Edison took a job with the Western Union telegraph in Boston. He won respect by taking down a message sent by the "fastest telegrapher in New York". But he was told off because his writing was too small. In anger, he filled each sheet of paper with a few huge words – and he was moved to another job.

At the age of 21, Edison read *Experimental Researches in Electricity* by the famous English scientist Michael Faraday. Like himself, Faraday was a self-taught scientist and experimenter with electricity. Edison was greatly encouraged. He began to write notebooks, take more care with his methods, and keep results of his experiments. He also visited the Boston workshops, where people were looking for new uses of electricity. Although various batteries and **dynamos** could make electricity, the telegraph was its only main use.

In 1868, Edison applied for his first patent, and it was granted the next year. It was for an **automatic** electrical vote counter, for US Congress meetings. But it was unsuccessful, because officials were reluctant to use it. Edison never forgot this lesson: do not bother with inventions that people will not want!

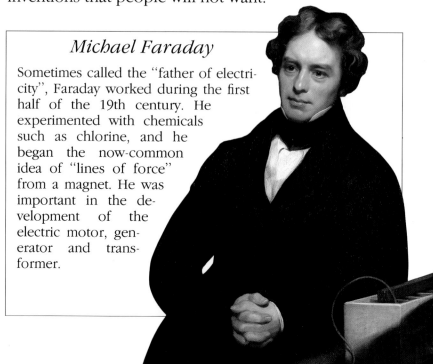

Michael Faraday

Sometimes called the "father of electricity", Faraday worked during the first half of the 19th century. He experimented with chemicals such as chlorine, and he began the now-common idea of "lines of force" from a magnet. He was important in the development of the electric motor, generator and transformer.

Chapter Two
The Budding Inventor

Edison realised that he wanted to work with electricity and machines. He wanted to invent and improve them. He left Western Union for the workshops of Charles Williams, a telegraph instrument maker. Here he invented his first successful machine, a stock ticker.

In the financial world, people buy **stocks and shares** in a company. This is like "lending" the company some money. If the company makes a profit, the people with its stocks and shares take some of it. Millions of dollars change hands. It is vital for such people to know which companies are doing well, and which shares are going up or down in price. Today this information is updated every second using computers, along telephone lines. In Edison's time messengers still ran from one office to another.

Edison's stock ticker was an adaptation of the telegraph. It sent the latest stock prices electrically along wires to printers in other offices. (Like the telegraph, it made a clicking or ticking sound as it worked.) As with much of Edison's work, it was an improvement on an old system, not a new idea.

The ticker-tape parade

When famous people visit New York and drive in an open car along the street, they are showered with pieces of paper. When this tradition started, the paper was paper tape from stock ticker machines. This is where the name "ticker-tape parade" came from.

A good earner

Edison's big chance came in the summer of 1869 when a new telegraphic machine that showed gold prices, at New York's Gold Exchange, broke down. Edison was asked to repair it. He repaired *and* improved the machine, so its owners, Western Union Telegraph Company, asked him to work on a new idea. The eventual result was the Edison Universal Stock Printer, the stock ticker.

An engraving of the Gold Room in New York City, where gold was bought and sold. Edison's stock ticker was used to communicate new prices for gold to other offices around New York.

Early business ventures

Leaving Boston, Edison went to New York and took a job in a gold recorder's office on Broad Street, in the city's financial centre. He worked on new systems for sending gold prices and stock prices between offices. The dealers who could get the latest prices fastest could make more money, by selling or buying ahead of their competitors.

But Edison was soon on the move again. He started a business with Franklin Pope, as Pope, Edison and Company, Electrical Engineers. They advertised that they could "devise electrical instruments and solve problems to order".

In one of his first big business deals, Edison earned $5,000 for selling his improved stock ticker and gold printer to Western Union. The same organization paid him the then enormous sum of $40,000 for an even better stock printer in 1870. One of the improvements was that a faulty or jammed printer could be restarted by sending special "unjamming" electrical signals along the wire.

With this great amount of money, Edison decided to set up a factory for making his inventions.

Edison's factory on Ward Street, Newark, New Jersey.

Chapter Three
Edison the Businessman

By 1871, Edison opened his own workshop and factory in Ward Street, Newark, New Jersey to manufacture stock tickers and other equipment, and to develop further electrical devices. He employed two shifts of workers and opened other workshops.

Edison worked incredibly hard. He took charge of all the projects, and he hardly slept. He expected his workers to do the same! Many did, because Edison set a good example. He showed great enthusiasm and kept up a stream of ideas on new devices.

He was not quite so successful in managing his business matters. He only opened a bank account to pay in the $40,000, and he stuck all his bills and payments on the wall with two nails!

The Edison family

On Christmas Day 1871, Edison married Mary Stilwell, a 16-year-old worker at his factory. Their first child, Marion, was born the next year. She was nicknamed Dot, from the dots-and-dashes of Morse code. In 1876, son Thomas was born – and nicknamed Dash! Another son, William, followed in 1878.

Mary Stilwell in the year of her marriage, aged 16.

11

Faster communications

For another payment of $40,000, Edison and his team worked for the Automatic Telegraph Company. For two years he worked on machines that eventually could transmit an accurate message at 200 words per minute – six times faster than the quickest telegraph operator. He went to England to sell the system to the Post Office there. While there he thought of trying to send messages across the Atlantic Ocean between the States and Britain, but tests that he did failed to work.

The telephone

In 1876, one of Edison's fellow inventors took out patents on a new device. Instead of sending dots and dashes or similar signals along a wire, it converted the sounds of the human voice into electrical signals and **transmitted** these. It was the first telephone, and its inventor was Alexander Graham Bell.

Rival companies realized how important the invention was. Edison was hired by Western Union to make a better version. He soon designed a system which used tiny granules of **carbon**, in a small container or "button". As the granules were pressed together by the sound waves of a voice, the amount of electricity passing through them varied. The carbon button telephone transmitter was successfully tested between New York and Philadelphia, and the patent was applied for in 1877. It was only given by the authorities after a long delay, in 1892. By that time Bell's system was well established.

Edison's designs for the carbon button telephone transmitter (left) and receiver (right). The transmitter changes the voice into electric signals and the receiver converts these back to a recognisable voice.

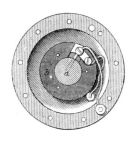
part of carbon transmitter

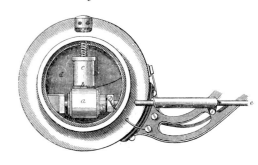
the inside of a receiver

Alexander Graham Bell speaking into the mouthpiece of his version of the telephone, which he patented in 1876.

Bell's telephone

Instead of carbon granules, Bell's telephone used the principle of electromagnetism. The sound waves hit a flat sheet, or diaphragm, of very thin metal and made it vibrate. As the diaphragm moved, this altered the magnetic field of a nearby magnet. In turn, the changing magnetic field created electrical signals in a coil of wire wrapped around the magnet. The electrical signals passed along the wire to the earpiece of the telephone at the other end, the prototype of which is shown here, where the whole process was reversed to make sound waves again.

Chapter Four

The Empire at Menlo Park

In 1876, Edison moved to Menlo Park, a village about 38 kilometres (24 miles) from New York City. He bought a house and built a large laboratory and workshop, including a machine shop for making parts, a carpenter's shop, and later a library. He gathered about 20 of his best workers around him. They were busy day and night, ate only when they were hungry, and slept only when they needed. They were carried along by the thrill of invention. Edison often slept at his desk.

Menlo Park was an "invention factory". Edison and his workers did not make instruments in large numbers, as at Ward Street. They left manufacturing to what Edison called the "robber barons" who bought patents from inventors for small sums, and made millions for themselves.

The team designed new machines and devices to solve specific problems. Ideas came to Edison all the time, and he made endless notes and sketches. At times he worked on 40 projects at once. In his working life he filled 3,400 notebooks!

Working hard.

Edison was known as a hard task master. He worked extremely hard and expected his employees to do the same. He himself summarised their working conditions by saying, "We don't pay anything and we work all the time." Once when a project was not working properly, he told his staff, "I've locked the door, and you'll have to stay here until this job is completed." He could get away with this because he himself worked hardest of all. In 1888, he spent a non-stop 72 hour stint working to improve the phonograph.

Towards the phonograph

In 1877, when Edison was working on his telephone system, he tried an experiment. The **diaphragm** of the telephone was a flat plate which vibrated when sound waves hit it. He tried to record its vibrations by linking it to a stylus (pen) pressing into paper. He rigged up a machine and recorded the word "halloo" as dents in the paper. When the marked paper was pulled back through, it moved the stylus, which vibrated the diaphragm, which produced sound waves in the air. As Edison said, with "strong imagination" the original word was heard again.

Edison was spurred on by reports that others were working on the same type of machine. He designed a machine with a recording cylinder covered not with paper, but with metal foil. This was built by his colleague John Kruesi in December 1877. It worked. One of Edison's first recordings on his new invention, the phonograph, was "Mary had a little lamb."

In 1878, Edison took his phonograph to the National Academy of Sciences.

Menlo Park was set up by Edison in 1876 and became one of the first invention factories, where inventors worked in teams to come up with new ideas and improvements. Later, Edison lit the grounds of Menlo Park with electric bulbs (see page 19).

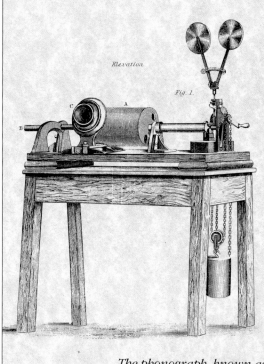

The phonograph

The principle of the phonograph (called the gramophone in Britain) remained the same for many years, but the machinery soon changed. Wax cylinders replaced the foil ones, and copies of the recording were made by moulding. But they soon wore out.

In 1887 a rival engineer, Emile Berliner, developed a recording made on a flat disc. The sound pattern was in a tiny wavy groove. The playback diaphragm became a big horn-shaped loudspeaker. The system was still mechanical – it did not use any electricity to amplify (make bigger) the vibrations or the sound signals. But the disc was more convenient, easier to copy, and gave better sound quality than Edison's version.

Gradually discs took over from cylinders, and became the LP (long-playing) record, made out of vinyl plastic. In 1912 Edison himself gave up with cylinders and used discs for his phonographs.

The phonograph, known as the talking machine, created a big stir. Edison enjoyed showing people what it could do and proving that it was not a big con.

Chapter Five

Let there be Light

A painting from the middle of the 19th century shows a family supper lit by an oil lamp.

In the 1870s, some houses had gas lights. Other people used candles or oil lamps – or they went to bed at dusk. The only electric lights were arc lights, where the glow came from an arc or "spark" of electricity jumping continuously between pieces of carbon. Some important buildings had arc lights. But they shone for only a few hours, then they had to be replaced. Also, they gave a very concentrated glare which was too bright to look at.

The glow-bulb

Edison visited the arc light exhibition of William Wallace, and took up the invention of a "safe, mild and inexpensive" electric lamp as his next target. Moreover, he intended to set up a system of electricity **generators** and wires and cables, like the gas pipe network, to bring electricity to everyone. He obtained money from businessmen and set up the Edison Electric Light Company.

In 1878 he applied for his first patent in the search for a "glow-bulb". It described a **filament** made of platinum, a hard metal that could withstand very high temperatures. There was also an electrical **governor** to prevent the platinum overheating.

Through the next year, work continued on the electric light. Meanwhile, Edison's nephew Charles took a new telephone receiver to London. It was demonstrated between the Royal Institution and the Royal Society. Workmen from the the rival Edison and Bell Telephone Companies were racing to lay wires across London, and they even **sabotaged** each other's work.

One per cent inspiration

Edison always admitted he was a "commercial inventor". He enjoyed scientific research, but not for its own sake. He wanted to devise things that would make people's lives easier – and which would make money. He realized that this meant long hours of patient observation and experiments, taking notes and trying alternatives. He might be helped by the occasional flash of insight. His famous saying was that "genius is one per cent inspiration, ninety-nine per cent perspiration".

When Edison turned his attention to the potential of electric lighting, he boasted that it would take him only six weeks to invent an electric light bulb that would not have all the disadvantages of arc lights. In fact it took him almost a year. The picture shows Edison and his co-workers in the laboratory at Menlo Park, working on the electric light bulb.

White-hot cotton

Edison and his team developed a new **vacuum** pump to make better vacuums in the glass bulbs. They also experimented with hundreds of materials for the filaments. They gave up with metal, and made one from specially treated carbonized cotton thread. Between 21 and 22 October 1879, the second of these new bulbs burned for 40 hours – a success! Edison at once applied for a patent. On New Year's Eve 1879 the Menlo Park streets and houses were lit with 30 of the new bulbs.

In London, the chemist and inventor Joseph Swan had been working along the same lines as Edison for 20 years. He also developed the carbon filament and vacuum bulb. Swan formed the Swan United Electric Light Company Limited. More battles over patents loomed, but in 1883 the Edison and Swan companies joined and the patent battle was solved.

In the meantime, Edison quickly applied for dozens of patents, mainly for electric lights, for the equipment used to make them, and for the distribution of electricity. (In his life he had a total of 1,093 patents.) The lamps themselves were continually improved. Bamboo fibres took the place of cotton, and years later **cellulose** was used.

The different designs for the light bulbs; one invented by Edison, one by Swan.

Making nothingness

In one type of vacuum pump, a piston sucks air out of the bulb through an open valve, while the valve to the air outside is closed. Then the piston moves back again, pushing the air out of the pump, while the valve to the bulb is shut. After many pumps, nearly all of the air is removed from the bulb.

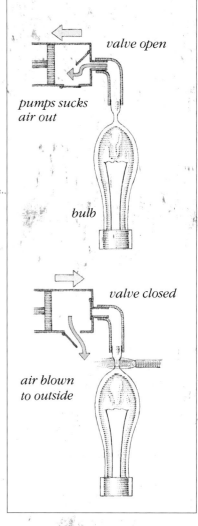

valve open

pumps sucks air out

bulb

valve closed

air blown to outside

Edison light bulb

Swan light bulb

The dynamo room in Edison's electric lighting station, 1882.

Power of the lights

If electric lamps were to light every home, Edison knew there had to be a system for making and distributing electricity. His team was soon working on this.

Business people rapidly realised that if they could light their offices and factories brightly, they could get far more work done, especially in the dark winter. Lighting systems were installed for newspaper offices and photographic companies, as well as private houses. The early ones were troublesome and needed many repairs, but they were quickly improved. By the early 1880s there were five electric light companies (including Edison's) trying to light up New York.

The first power station

Edison now looked at the source of the electricity itself – the **dynamo** or generator. He improved existing designs to make them twice as efficient, at turning the energy in their fuel into electrical energy. His team provided lighting for the first French Electrical Exposition in Paris. With his business hat on, Edison set up electric light companies in France, England, Italy, Holland and Belgium.

The year of 1882 was a milestone. The Edison company exhibited an artistic lighting display at the Crystal Palace in London. More than 100,000 electric lamps were made in the USA, to satisfy the rocketing demand.

Edison and his advisers found premises for the manufacture of dynamos, lamps and cables. They also chose a site for the world's first real power station and the area to be served by it, in Manhattan, New York. This was Pearl Street, where Edison's power station and electricity system were switched on in September 1882.

Soon afterwards, the first electricity to be generated from the energy of running water was produced at Appleby, Wisconsin. It used the flow of the Fox River. Despite great success, and more power stations, and more electric light systems, Edison's money kept running out. Some was lost due to poor business methods, and the rest was spent on yet more inventions.

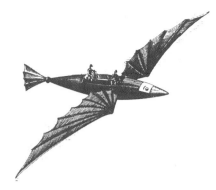

Edison's creative vision sensed that many things could be possible. For example, he imagined flying machines like the one above or others more like helicopters. However, it was other inventors of that time who pursued these dreams.

Family tragedy

In 1884 Edison's wife Mary died of typhoid. On top of this tragedy, in the following year he began the first of more than 200 legal battles to stop others copying his lighting equipment. This took nearly ten years and cost him $2,000,000. In the meantime he looked at the possibilities of making a flying machine (today we would call it a helicopter), but he was badly burned in an accident and gave up.

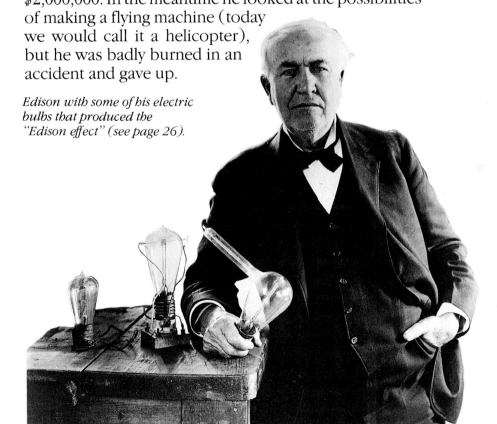

Edison with some of his electric bulbs that produced the "Edison effect" (see page 26).

Chapter Six
A New Life

Two years after Mary's death, Edison married again. His second wife was Mina Miller, and they had three children, Madeleine, Charles and Theodore. Edison decided it was time for change. He was now a famous businessman, and he was less able to spend long hours in the laboratory. He bought Glenmont, a house at West Orange, New Jersey, and built laboratories, workshops and factories ten times bigger than Menlo Park.

Edison and his teams worked on an improved phonograph with a floating stylus, an electric motor and wax cylinders. The West Orange factory made dolls with tiny phonographs inside them, which played nursery rhymes.

Edison was now a world figure. He met heads-of-state and famous scientists in Europe, founded a recording company, and developed a dictaphone (a small machine for recording speech, to be typed later).

Mina Edison and daughter Madeleine. She was 19 when she married Edison.

The Edisons' new home, Glenmont, in West Orange, New Jersey. Here, Mina was able to make sure that Thomas spent more time with his family and not so much at work.

An advertisement for the Edison talking doll, an example of one of the uses the phonograph was put to in 1890.

WE ARE NOW PREPARED
TO SUPPLY THE

EDISON TALKING DOLL

EDISON'S
TALKING DOLL.

TO THE TRADE
ONLY.

For Wholesale Price and Terms, Address

EDISON PHONOGRAPH TOY MFG. CO.,

No. 138 FIFTH AVENUE,
NEW YORK.

The photographer Eadweard Muybridge came to West Orange to demonstrate his "moving pictures". He and Edison discussed the possibility of linking recorded pictures to the recorded voice. In 1888, Edison took out patents on his **kinetoscope**, an early piece of movie equipment. A co-worker William Dickson showed him a movie picture with sound – one of the earliest "talkies". But the equipment had problems, and the Edison team went on to other projects. Real talkies did not begin until 1927.

Eadweard Muybridge, an English photographer, was famous for his studies of animal motion.

The birth of motion pictures

Edison is sometimes said to have invented motion pictures, the movie camera and the movie projector.

In fact, they were the work of several people, including members of his companies.

● Eadweard Muybridge showed the idea was feasible, with his pictures of running horses.

● Edison's work colleague William Dickson first tried to record the pictures on wax cylinders.

● Then Dickson used the new flexible celluloid film, devised by George Eastman, for the **kinetograph** and kinetoscope.

● In 1893 Black Maria, the world's first movie studio, was set up at Glenmont. Kinetoscopes were installed in New York to show the resulting films.

● Edison did not think the kinetograph and kinetoscope would become hugely successful, so he did not protect them by patents in Europe.

● In the 1890s in France, Louis and Auguste Lumière further improved Edison's machines. Soon there were dozens of inventors working on improved versions of motion picture cameras and projectors.

Edison's laboratory at West Orange. It shows the inside of the kinetographic theatre with a phonograph and kinetograph being used at the same time to achieve a film with sound.

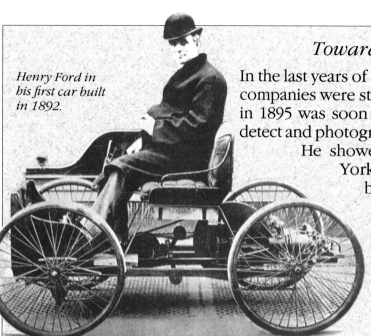

Henry Ford in his first car built in 1892.

Towards the 20th century

In the last years of the 19th century, Edison and his companies were still busy. The discovery of X-rays in 1895 was soon followed by a better screen to detect and photograph them – designed by Edison. He showed the "fluoroscopes" in New York, where people could view their bones! He rushed through new versions of a movie film projector and talking pictures. A man called Henry Ford, a worker in one of Edison's companies, built his first and second automobiles. He was later to become the founder of the Ford Motor company.

Radio and electronics

Edison's storage battery that was able to power a car. It was completed in 1902.

The 20th century saw the first "wire-less" radio messages sent across the Atlantic Ocean, by Guglielmo Marconi. Edison sent his congratulations, sold Marconi his patent on wireless telegraphy from 1885, and said: "That fellow's work puts him in my class." The great era of radio and electronics was beginning. Edison lacked knowledge about the details of how electricity really worked, and he was too busy with his big industrial projects to get involved.

For many years, Edison worked on electrical cells more commonly called batteries. He invented the **alkaline** storage battery, which could be recharged. In 1912, Edison and Nikola Tesla (who once worked for him) were offered the Nobel prize for Physics. Tesla refused to share the prize, so it was awarded to physicist Nils Gustaf Dalen.

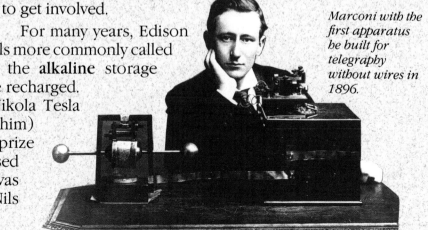

Marconi with the first apparatus he built for telegraphy without wires in 1896.

The Last Years

One of Edison's last projects was to find an alternative source of rubber to the British-owned rubber plantations. He wanted American rubber-using industries to be independent. After breeding many new types of plants, he came up with a type of giant goldenrod (a common flower) that produced latex rubber. But others were working on artificial rubber, and the goldenrod rubber never went into production.

Apart from his deafness, Edison had always enjoyed good health, despite his hundreds of late-night sessions in the laboratory. In 1929 Henry Ford organised a celebration of 50 years of electric lights, with a new Museum of History which contained the rebuilt laboratory from Menlo Park. Edison attended the celebrations with US President Herbert Hoover. He was 82. After this, his health began to fail.

Through 1930-1, Edison fought illness. In his last public message he said: "I have lived a long time ... Have faith. Go forward." He died on 18 October 1931, after suffering from **diabetes** and a kidney problem called Bright's disease.

The First World War

When World War One began in Europe in 1914, Edison suggested that the armed forces should have a research laboratory to develop better weapons. He became chairman of the Navy Consulting Board, which had members from the best research organizations in America. He imagined a war where soldiers worked killing machines rather than fighting each other hand-to-hand. As busy as ever, he also developed torpedo-detecting devices, like underwater telephones, and anti-submarine devices.

Above, Edison naps during one of his camping trips with President Harding and Harvey Firestone (one of the leading manufacturers of rubber tyres) in 1921.

Edison in his later years.

The commercial side of Edison's style of practical science is shown in this amazing advertisement for light bulbs.

Chapter Seven
Edison in perspective

Edison's inventions and improvements were only part of his great contribution to modern life, which ranged through electrical engineering and chemistry, to transport, entertainment and the comforts of daily living.

Edison himself was a "rags to riches" story. He had little proper schooling in science or business. Yet through good sense, a busy and questioning mind, and sheer hard work, he gained fame and fortune. He applied for a patent on average every two weeks of his working life.

Research and development

The teams and working methods which Edison set up at Menlo Park were the first of their kind. Other organizations soon followed the idea of bringing together experts in different branches of science, to carry out experiments and work together in a step-by-step way on new projects. Today we call these activities "research and development". No major company can expect to progress without them.

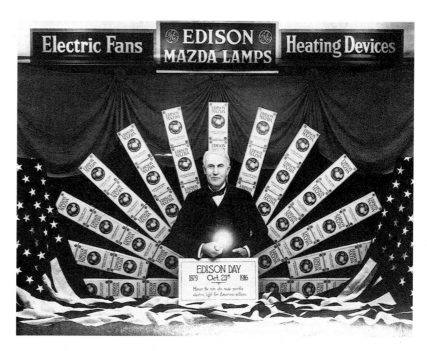

A scientist at heart

Edison's notebooks show that he understood many of the principles of science, despite his lack of training. He also followed the scientific method – having ideas, testing them, analysing and explaining the results, and moving on to the next stage.

Edison was partly an old-time inventor, who loved working long hours in the laboratory. And he was partly a modern businessman, setting up teams of experts and putting profits from his companies back into research. When he was born, at the time of the candle and oil lamp, the world was in the "dark ages". By his death, the modern age of machines and technology and electronics had begun.

On 21 October 1931 the entire American nation paid tribute to the "Wizard of Menlo Park" at his funeral. They switched off their lights and shut down their electrical equipment. For one minute only, the whole of America was dark – imagine New York with no lights on! The lights have never been off since and the magnificence of New York at night is one of Edison's legacies to us today.

The World in Edison's Time

	1847-1875	1876-1900
Science	**1847** Thomas Edison is born **1852** Biologist Hermann Helmholtz measures the speed of a nerve signal, in a frog's leg **1861** Physicist James Maxwell makes the first colour photograph	**1883** The USA is divided into four time zones, as suggested by the railroad companies **1893** Rudolf Diesel works on the first internal combustion engine, which will be named after him
Exploration	**1853** First railway lines and telegraph cables laid in India **1853** Van Diemen's Land, an island off the south-east of Australia, is officially renamed Tasmania after its first European visitor, Abel Tasman, who sailed there in 1642-43	**1888** Scandinavian explorer Fridtjof Nansen and his team complete the first land crossing of Greenland
Politics	**1848** Karl Marx and Friedrich Engels write *Communist Manifesto* **1861** American Civil War begins **1865** US President Abraham Lincoln shot dead while watching a play at the theatre	**1891** In Britain, the Factory Act forbids children under 11 years old to work in factories any more **1894** Japan and China go to war, again **1899** Boer War begins in southern Africa
Arts	**1860s** French painter Claude Monet begins to produce his most famous works, known as impressionistic paintings **1873** French author Jules Verne writes *Around the World in 80 Days*	**1879** A young Spanish girl and her father discover the now-famous prehistoric cave paintings at Altamira, Spain **1896** Chemist Alfred Nobel dies, and the five annual Nobel Prizes for physics, chemistry, medicine, literature and peace are founded

1901-1925	1925-1950
1903 Wilbur and Orville Wright make the first heavier-than-air aeroplane flight	**1928** Scottish microbiologist Alexander Fleming discovers a mould that makes a substance he calls penicillin – the first antibiotic drug
1905 Albert Einstein begins his work on the theory of relativity	
	1931 Thomas Edison dies
1912 Nils Dalen of Sweden, inventor of gas regulators for lighthouses, wins the Nobel Prize for Physics	**1948** An American team invents the transistor
1902 The first telegraph cable is laid under the Pacific	**1927** American aviator Charles Lindberg makes the first non-stop trans-Atlantic solo flight, in *Spirit of St Louis*
1905 The Cullinan diamond, the world's largest, is found in South Africa	
	1947 A huge meteorite falls in remote Siberia, devastating countryside for a great area
1911 Roald Amundsen is the first to reach the South Pole	
1914 World War One begins	**1939** World War Two begins
1917 The Russian Revolution begins	**1945** World War Two ends
1918 World War One ends	**1948** In the Middle East, the new Jewish state named Israel is established
1922 Civil War ends in Russia	
1904 Anton Chekhov, Russian playwright, finishes *The Cherry Orchard*	**1928** English author D H Lawrence writes *Lady Chatterley's Lover,* which was banned in Britain until 1960
1911 Composer Irving Berlin writes an early jazz song, *Alexander's Ragtime Band*	
	1930 Marlene Dietrich stars in her first well-known movie, *The Blue Angel*
1912 Edgar Rice Burroughs publishes the first of his *Tarzan of the Apes* stories	

Glossary

alkaline: in chemistry, the opposite of acidic. An alkaline substance usually feels greasy or slippery, and strong alkalis can be damaging. An alkaline substance reacts with an acid to form a chemical salt.

automatic: something which happens on its own, by itself, instead of being controlled by a person or another device. For example, an automatic level-crossing barrier at a railway crossing comes down across the road as a train approaches, without the need for a person to operate it.

carbon: a natural substance that occurs in many forms, from diamonds to coal, coke, charcoal and soot. Solid carbon (which makes up a lot of the "lead" in a pencil) lets a certain amount of electricity pass through it. Carbon granules are small, black specks, rather like soot.

cellulose: a natural substance made by plants, which is often long and stringy. The cellulose of some plants, such as cotton or flax, is woven together to make cloth.

diabetes: a medical condition in which the body cannot use its natural sugars properly. Untreated, diabetes may cause drowsiness, unconsciousness or even death. Treatments include eating certain foods at the correct times, special tablets, and injections of a substance called insulin.

diaphragm: a flat flexible sheet or plate, often made of very thin metal, which usually can move to and fro, or shake, or vibrate. The part of a loudspeaker that moves to and fro, making sound waves, is sometimes called the diaphragm.

dynamo: a machine for making electricity, usually direct current (DC) electricity. See *generator.*

engineering: the science of designing, making, putting together and maintaining machines and structures, from a pair of scissors to a jumbo jet.

filament: a long, thin part or structure, such as the thin piece of wire that glows in an electric light bulb, or a single strand of a substance such as nylon.

generator: a machine that makes electricity from some other form of energy, such as the heat given off by burning coal or oil, or the power of rushing water, or nuclear fuel, or the heat or light of the Sun in solar power. A *dynamo* makes direct current electricity (DC), an alternator makes alternating current (AC).

governor: in engineering, a device that controls or limits the movements of part of a machine. In a steam engine, the governor controls the turning speed of the flywheel at the most efficient rate, so that it does not rotate too fast or too slow.

kinetograph: an early type of movie or motion-picture, developed by Thomas Edison. It did not take photographs as clearly or as quickly as later cameras. It was named from the word "kinetic", which means "moving" or "in motion".

kinetoscope: an early piece of movie or motion-picture equipment, a "peep-hole" machine, developed by Thomas Edison. It was a large box containing a long roll of movie film that went round and round, watched by one person through a hole or binocular-type eyepieces. See also *kinetograph.*

legal: to do with the laws and rules of company, organization or country.

Morse code: a code of short electrical signals (dots) and long ones (dashes), that spell out letters and words. For example, the letter S is dot-dot-dot. It was invented by American Samuel Morse in about 1838, for use on the *telegraph* system.

philosophy: the study of human knowledge, beliefs and thoughts. It affects many aspects of our lives, such as how we know things, why we believe in right and wrong, and why we think some things are valuable but others are worthless.

sabotaged: having interfered with or disrupted something, so that it goes wrong or breaks.

stocks and shares: a sort of "share" or "part ownership" in a company or organization, in return for putting money into the company. Shares usually give the owner, or shareholder, a say in the running of the company, and a share in the profits made by the company.

telegraph: a device for sending messages over long distances along electrical wires, usually in the form of a code such as on-off signals or the dots and dashes of *Morse code.*

transmit: to send or beam out. A television satellite transmits TV signals to the Earth from space, and a *telegraph* transmits electrical signals along a wire.

vacuum: nothingness – a place where there is nothing, not even air. Most of Space is a vacuum. It is not generally possible to have a perfect vacuum, where there really is nothing at all. There are usually a few tiny specks of gas or other substances floating about.

Index